National Audit Office

AF824422

HM Treasury

Spending Review 2015

Report by the Comptroller and Auditor General

Ordered by the House of Commons
to be printed on 20 July 2016

This report has been prepared under Section 6 of the National Audit Act 1983 for presentation to the House of Commons in accordance with Section 9 of the Act

Sir Amyas Morse KCB
Comptroller and Auditor General
National Audit Office

19 July 2016

HC 571 | £10.00

This study examines whether the spending review is an effective mechanism for planning and allocating public money in the medium term.

11212 07/16 NAO

Contents

The National Audit Office study team consisted of:
Jonathan Bayliss, Sudip Dasgupta, Benoit Guerin, Sian Jones and Sarah Pearcey, under the direction of Keith Davis.

This report can be found on the National Audit Office website at www.nao.org.uk

For further information about the National Audit Office please contact:

National Audit Office
Press Office
157–197 Buckingham Palace Road
Victoria
London
SW1W 9SP

Tel: 020 7798 7400

Enquiries: www.nao.org.uk/contact-us

Website: www.nao.org.uk

Twitter: @NAOorguk

Preface

Planning and management in government: the need for a new framework

This report and *Government's management of its performance: progress with single departmental plans* cover two key elements of the way government plans and manages its business.[1] This has led us to consider how the processes fit within an overarching strategic framework.

In the National Audit Office's view there are significant weaknesses in the framework for planning and managing public sector activity in the UK. A set of processes and guidance has been established within government, but in our view it does not represent a coherent, integrated system. This means that the way government plans and manages its business is driven by processes, for example the process by which HM Treasury negotiates with and allocates funding to departments, rather than an overarching strategic framework for achieving government's objectives and achieving an appropriate balance between short-term political drivers and long-term value for money.

As departments attempt to redesign planning around single departmental plans there is now an opportunity for government to articulate and commit to an enduring framework for strategic business planning and management. Against this background, the two reports should be considered together, as the allocation of resources and the monitoring of their performance are inextricably linked.

Challenges facing government

Government currently faces significant challenges in providing public services, which means there is now a greater need than ever before for an effective strategic business planning and management framework. The challenges include:

- **Continued austerity**. Departments are being asked to do more with less; to do so successfully requires a deep understanding of what they currently achieve with what they currently have.

- **Managing transformation**. Many departments are planning to do things differently. This creates uncertainty in how they manage what they do, as well as substantial change or investment programmes to manage as they move from A to B.

1 Comptroller and Auditor General, *Government's management of its performance: progress with single departmental plans*, Session 2016-17, HC 872, National Audit Office, July 2017.

- **Devolution**. Moving to a devolved model, both across the nations of the UK and in terms of English service delivery, changes responsibility for delivering particular services, and the role of central government departments – and generates additional tensions in how spending and performance is tracked.
- **Capacity**. Government is trying to do all this with a smaller staff base and management capacity, particularly in the centre of departments, owing to the spending reductions which have already occurred.
- **Complexity**. Many of the issues government is trying to tackle require a response which cuts across traditional departmental boundaries or services.

Pervasive problems in government

In our work, we have repeatedly found that problems in the delivery of public services can be traced back to the way in which government makes decisions about how to implement policy. This led us to diagnose, ahead of the general election in 2015, four pervasive problems affecting service delivery. These pervasive problems stem from the lack of an effective management framework:

- **Ignoring inconvenient facts:** Departments often make decisions on poor or incomplete information, leading to poor value for money and service failure.
- **Out of sight out of mind:** Making decisions without understanding the consequences, particularly if these fall in another area of government or in the future.
- **Not learning from previous mistakes:** Having no adequate mechanism for challenge and action, or learning from good practice. Project monitoring is not good enough to identify problems in time.
- **Conflicting priorities:** The lack of a clear understanding of aims and a clear achievable plan for how to attain them.

Our work on *Managing business operations – what government needs to get right* has assessed government's maturity across five domains of operational management; strategy, information, people, process, and improvement.[2] It shows that government has weaknesses across all domains, and that a more integrated management approach is necessary to achieve real, sustainable service improvements.

2 National Audit Office, *Managing business operations – what government needs to get right*, September 2015.

Need for a strong framework

Government needs a proper framework for planning to the medium term and beyond, that will allow it to make achievable plans, and to understand what it needs to know to stay on track. This framework should be stable and enduring, existing independent of political priorities – whatever your objectives, there are some fundamentals you will need to allow you to plan and manage effectively, even (or perhaps especially) as you change priorities.

A robust management framework is also likely to be a strong basis for providing both civil service accountability to ministers for results, and accountability to Parliament and the public for government's use of taxpayers' money. Our work on the state of accountability to Parliament highlighted barriers to the frank and realistic discussion of plans and performance, between civil servants and ministers, which are necessary for successful delivery of reforms. It is therefore in the interests of both politicians and civil servants to commit to a framework that supports those discussions.[3]

Various parts of the centre of government have set out processes and guidance for different elements of planning and managing its business, from the principles and practice of managing public money, to option appraisal and corporate governance. Key processes also include periodic spending reviews and the new single departmental plans, as well as the ongoing 'business as usual' engagements between HM Treasury spending teams and departments. Within their own terms some of these processes – such as the spending review – are acknowledged to be strong in comparison to practice elsewhere. These processes also continue to be enhanced – for example the guidance on managing major projects has been significantly improved in recent years.

The view of government is that these individual processes together provide a management system, albeit with room for improvement. However, it is our view that this collection of processes does not amount to the coherent strategic framework for planning and managing public sector activity that is needed, and that without such a framework the way government plans and manages its business will not be able to tackle the pervasive problems it faces.

This problem is not unique to the United Kingdom. Governments across the world are grappling with how to manage large programmes and drive real progress in delivering outcomes. There are some examples of good practice across the world that the UK can look to, which demonstrate strong links between planning, budgeting, monitoring and intervention, and clear expectations for delivering outcomes.

3 Comptroller and Auditor General, *Accountability to Parliament for taxpayers' money*, Session 2015-16, HC 849, National Audit Office, February 2016.

A possible framework for effective strategic business planning and management

The framework we have developed sets out our expectations of strategic business planning and management at the centre of government. It is based on the standard management cycle and incorporates findings from our work, and from international good practice (**Figure 1**). We see a need for government to work towards adopting such a framework, thereby moving to a greater level of maturity than the current approach which is overly disconnected and process-led. We see this as crucial if government is to successfully deliver the objectives and achieve the transformation it aspires to, while ensuring value for taxpayers' money.

Figure 1

A framework for strategic business planning and management

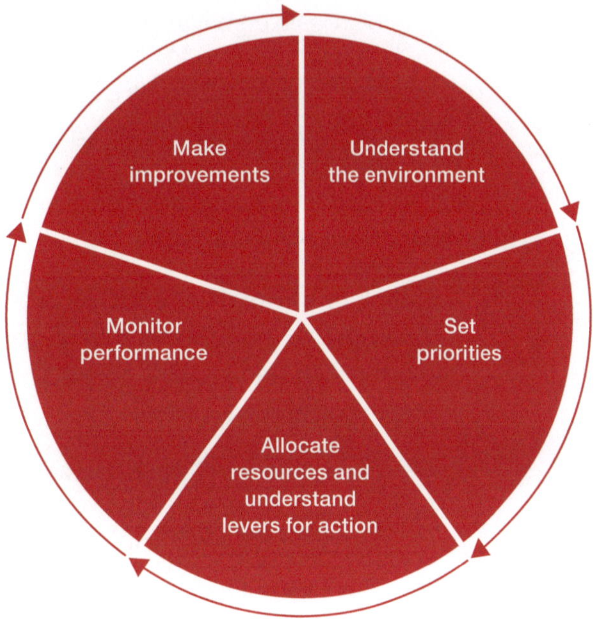

Note

1 This framework is based on the standard management cycle, which we have used in previous reports as a framework for reviewing specific projects and programmes. We have enhanced the framework to reflect the more strategic viewpoint of these reports, as well as our previous work on accountability and the centre of government.

Source: National Audit Office analysis

This framework, which should operate in a cyclical way, with continuous feedback and adjustment, would allow any new government to know what the baselines of performance and spending are, redefine objectives and reallocate resources according to its priorities, and quickly start to monitor progress, adjusting performance indicators or targets where necessary. The framework has six key elements:

a **Understanding the environment**. Numerous factors will have an impact on what government does and how it does it – departments may not control these but must seek to understand them as part of *strategic planning*, and continue to monitor them as they change over time. These include:

- The demand for services.
- Legal and other commitments.
- The fiscal landscape.
- Manifesto commitments.
- Stated policy/delivery preferences.
- The current business model.

These will have an ongoing effect on all parts of the framework and should not be considered as a one-off exercise.

b **Setting priorities**. The centre of government works with departments on *strategic planning* which sets the direction of government, including the relative importance of competing (and possibly conflicting) objectives. To do this, it must have fully understood and articulated:

- the challenges it is trying to address and outcomes it wishes to see;
- the constraints there are on government's ability to act; and
- the options it has to address those challenges.

c **Understanding levers for action**. To move from high-level decisions about priorities to *business planning*, the government must understand how the different levers for action will affect the outcomes it is trying to achieve. This will include what stakeholders within and outside government are involved, how any change in delivery model will affect the resources needed, and the relative value for money of different options.

d **Allocating resources**. HM Treasury is responsible for high level *business planning* – allocating the resources each programme or project will receive, considering any trade-offs or prioritisation which needs to be made. This covers not only their funding, but also the capacity and capability of the staff, and must be based on a detailed understanding of what resources government has, and different ways in which they can be deployed – the levers for action. Departments have responsibility in a similar way for lower level *business planning*.

e **Monitoring performance**. An effective performance measurement and reporting system is essential to the framework – it provides the information that powers the cycle and keeps it running. Performance information is essential for management to know if it is on track, correct and improve. It is also essential to provide *accountability* to the key stakeholders who ultimately provide the authority to act/spend money – in the case of government, this means Parliament and the public. The information required to monitor performance covers:

- Inputs (money and other resources).
- Outputs delivered and enabling actions achieved, as well as direct measures of outcomes.
- While specific targets for service levels or outcomes may not be desired, it is important to clearly set out what constitutes 'success' – so that any mismatch with expectations can be identified and corrected.
- For longer-term goals, both leading and lagging indicators are needed to ensure performance is on trajectory.

f **Making improvements**. Based on what the performance information is showing, there must be effective mechanisms, to correct underperformance, adjust and reallocate resources if necessary. Government should also have a way to review priorities, resources, actions and performance measures, and make changes if they are no longer valuable.

This framework covers both financial and performance management, and we believe that the two are equally important in successfully managing government. We (and the Committee of Public Accounts) have commented repeatedly on the historical disconnect between financial and performance management across government. The split is apparent from the highest level downwards.

Our report

This report focuses on the Spending Review 2015, which set out the high-level financial plans for departments. It is published alongside *Government's management of performance – progress with single departmental plans*, which examines how departments are using the introduction of single departmental plans as a new approach to business planning and performance management. These two reports examine two of the key elements of the way government currently plans and manages its business, and we report on the extent to which they meet the expectations set for them, and our previous recommendations.

Taken together, while these two reports demonstrate that government has made some progress, they lead us to the view expressed at the start, that the current approach amounts to a collection of top-down, set-piece processes and guidance that fail to make the most of the understanding and expertise across government, and not the overarching integrated framework for strategic business planning and management that government needs. Without making a shift to such a framework, government cannot hope to optimise value for taxpayers' money or deliver continuous performance improvement.

This is not easy – improving practice has taken other countries a significant amount of time and effort. We do not underestimate the challenge for the UK, given the scale and complexity of government, as well as it being a time of transition in terms of devolution and exit from the European Union. But that is not an excuse not to start.

Key facts

£21.5bn	£1,875bn	40
reductions announced at Spending Review, to the budgets of unprotected departments, of which £9.5 billion will be reinvested	total amount of DEL spending set by the Spending Review 2015 for 2016-17 to 2020-21	entities with an individual settlement

18	weeks between the formal launch of the Spending Review 2015 and the final announcement of settlements
2	formal joint bids
92%	of finance directors we surveyed who felt that HM Treasury had managed some or all aspects of the Spending Review process well

Summary

Background to spending reviews

1 The spending review is a key political and fiscal event that attracts widespread parliamentary and public interest. HM Treasury carries out spending reviews to allocate funding across the government's priorities, set limits on spending and define the main outcomes that the public can expect the government to achieve with its resources. It is the government's major tool in planning medium-term expenditure and an opportunity to reform the way services are provided.

2 Taxpayers have a right to expect that decisions taken in spending reviews are based not only on government policy commitments, but also on robust data about how much the different options cost and whether these options will enable the government to achieve its goals. Spending should be prioritised rationally across the government as a whole. Spending reviews should act as both a spending control, setting limits on departments, and as a way of maximising value for money. Once spending reviews are complete, departments use their formal settlements to set the parameters for more detailed budgeting and planning.

3 The Spending Review 2015 allocated almost £2 trillion in departmental spending, and another £2 trillion in welfare and benefits payments, over five years. It also announced that the government would make £21.5 billion of spending cuts. It was a significant logistical exercise, involving a wide range of teams across HM Treasury, departments and other stakeholders.

4 The spending review is one of the main ways for the centre of government to work with departments to set the government's overall strategy. It is used to ensure that public expenditure is controlled in support of the government's fiscal framework. These controls should also be used to provide incentives for departments to manage spending well, to provide high-quality public services that offer value for money to the taxpayer. Our previous work has raised concerns about whether departments and the centre do enough to plan and manage the change the government undertakes. This report assesses the Spending Review 2015 within that context.

5 As set out in the Preface, government needs a stable and enduring framework, existing independent of political priorities, for planning to the medium-term and beyond, that will allow it to make achievable plans, and to understand what it needs to know to stay on track. This is not an easy issue for the centre of government to deal with. The structures of public sector accountability make working between departments difficult, and political realities mean that long-term thinking is not always a priority. Moving away from this will require a cultural change in departments, as well as in the centre of government. However, getting financial and performance measurement right, within a framework that is well-established and well-understood, is crucial to achieving objectives.

Scope of our report

6 Our report examines whether the spending review is effective as a medium-term spending and planning tool. It looks at:

- the importance of the spending review process;
- the extent to which the Spending Review 2015 took account of the key principles needed to make well-informed decisions; and
- the relationships and processes that HM Treasury and departments have in place to achieve effective outcomes.

7 We focus on how the spending review process enables the government to make sound, evidence-based decisions, rather than on the decisions themselves. We have not evaluated the quality of departments' bids. Instead, we have focused on the systems HM Treasury has in place to request, understand and challenge evidence within the bids.

Key findings

Importance of spending reviews

8 Spending reviews help ensure that departments have certainty about how much government funding they will receive, and provide an opportunity to budget and plan for multiple years. The spending review process is set up to support control of public expenditure, and there is a close correlation between spending review settlements and subsequent spend. Departments we interviewed said that the spending review process is effective in setting funding over a parliamentary term. We found that Budgets provided year-on-year flexibility to enable departments to respond to changing priorities (paragraphs 1.1 to 1.4).

9 **HM Treasury has made some incremental progress following National Audit Office and Committee of Public Accounts reports, but these improvements have not gone as far as we would have expected.** This report builds on our previous work, including our reports *Managing budgeting in government*, and *Financial management in government*.[4] These reports examined opportunities to achieve better value for money and risks arising from the way the spending review process is undertaken. We have followed up progress on the recommendations from the Committee of Public Accounts' 2013 report.[5] This shows that while HM Treasury has made some progress, such as working with departments to understand the models and assumptions which underpinned bids, the pace and scale of improvement has been limited (paragraphs 1.9 to 1.10 and Appendix Three).

10 **Spending Reviews provide weak incentives for departments to demonstrate how they will achieve value for money.** Our *Managing budgeting in government* report found that the budgetary system addresses the Treasury's objectives for prioritisation and value for money less effectively than objectives relating to spending control.[6] We have drawn on this and other previous reports, and those of the Committee of Public Accounts, to design a set of principles that set out what a 'good' spending review process would look like. These include the importance of strong evidence, both to support decisions and to monitor performance; the need for clear long-term and cross-departmental views of spending; and the need to understand the capability and capacity of departments to deliver their plans. Our key findings are set out against these principles (paragraphs 11 to 21 and 1.11).

Principle 1

Evidence to support decisions

Robust evidence is essential to understand whether the government is achieving value for money, to make fair comparisons to prioritise spending and to redesign services.

Our 2012 report, *Managing budgeting in government*, found that "the data required to inform decision-makers on optimal resource allocation was not readily available and in some places did not exist".

11 **HM Treasury took steps to understand the evidence base that underpinned departmental forecasts and baseline models before the start of the Spending Review.** Both HM Treasury's spending teams and the departments thought this activity helped them to develop a good level of mutual understanding. The Department for Transport, for example, began its preparations about 18 months before the start of the Spending Review, and engaged with Treasury on its policy and delivery options. It also allowed the Spending Review to focus more on specific spending decisions, since forecasts and baselines had already been shared. HM Treasury also carried out some specific cross-departmental reviews of spending, for example on capital projects and on pay. These helped it to provide more consistent evidence across government (paragraphs 2.2 to 2.5 and 2.9).

4 Comptroller and Auditor General, *Managing budgeting in government*, Session 2012-13, HC 597, National Audit Office, October 2012; and Comptroller and Auditor General, *Financial management in government*, Session 2013-14, HC 131, National Audit Office, June 2013.

5 HC Committee of Public Accounts, *Managing budgeting in government*, Thirty-fourth Report of Session 2012-13, HC 661, February 2013.

6 Comptroller and Auditor General, *Managing budgeting in government*, Session 2012-13, HC 597, National Audit Office, October 2012.

12 Other tools that HM Treasury intended to deliver as part of the Financial Management Review were not sufficiently developed to be a valuable part of the Spending Review 2015 process. One aim of the Financial Management Review was to develop tools, particularly for costing and understanding the value of service delivery, which would help inform spending reviews. The original plan was for these tools to be rolled out to all departments in 2015, in preparation for a possible spending review in the autumn. However, both HM Treasury and departments acknowledge that the tools were not detailed enough and not completed consistently across departments. HM Treasury did, however, make use of the Planning and Performance committee, set up as part of the Financial Management Review, to help prepare finance staff in departments (paragraphs 2.6 to 2.9).

Principle 2

An integrated view across organisational boundaries

The need to tackle complex issues to achieve outcomes requires a cross-departmental approach. Departments need to collaborate and to understand the links between services.

Our 2012 report, *Managing budgeting in government,* found that "The budgetary system does not incentivise departments to collaborate ... There are some promising developments in departments, which could be built on."

13 HM Treasury has not addressed problems with the spending review structure, which is not well suited to deal with issues that increasingly span departmental boundaries. Our 2012 report recommended that "spending teams ... identify opportunities for departments to gain from working together and encourage them to do so". However, the process remains largely bilateral, with individual departments submitting information to individual spending teams (paragraphs 3.2 and 3.3).

14 HM Treasury recognises the importance of joint working, but has found it challenging to encourage departments to submit formal joint bids. HM Treasury informed us only two formal joint bids were received – the same number as in 2010. This approach does not link with key cross-government objectives, such as those of the Cabinet implementation taskforces. Departments told us there were a range of reasons why they did not submit joint bids. These included political disagreements, a lack of clarity about policy and budgetary responsibility, and insufficient flexibility in planning across government to enable them to work with other departments (paragraphs 3.3 to 3.5).

15 **Some departments did work together on specific themes across the 2015 Spending Review process.** Departments worked together on a range of initiatives. The Department for Education and the Department for Business, Innovation & Skills set up a joint working team on apprenticeships. HM Revenue & Customs and the Department for Work & Pensions agreed common assumptions on overlap in benefit claimants. Where these initiatives work, there may be no need for a formal joint bid. However, without a formal joint bid there may be limits to the accountability of such arrangements (paragraphs 3.6 and 3.7).

Principle 3

A longer-term view

Decisions about spending and how services are provided can have long-term effects on public finances and outcomes. These effects need to be considered when assessing value for money.

Our 2012 report, *Managing budgeting in government*, found that "The UK budgetary process does not include the sort of longer-term vision seen in other countries and could help inform strategic decision-making."

16 **The Spending Review 2015 focused on funding decisions until the end of the Parliament, meaning there was less focus on the long term.** Although many government projects take years to achieve their aims, the exercise to review proposed capital expenditure shows that spending review submissions are strongly skewed towards what is achievable in the spending review period. Only 47 out of 458 (10%) capital bids indicated that they would likely need capital funding past 2020-21, of which 29 bids (6%) were quantified. Some departments have specific long-term needs, such as the Department for Transport's roads strategy or the 30-year devolution deals managed by the Department for Communities and Local Government. HM Treasury considered these, but they did not form part of the standard business of the Spending Review (paragraphs 4.2 and 4.3 and 4.5 to 4.7).

17 **The Spending Review's consideration of impacts also had a short-term focus.** Spending review decisions may have potential unintended consequences, such as making immediate cost savings that result in higher costs in the future, shifting costs to consumers, or moving operations to the private sector. Some nine out of 13 finance directors who responded to the question in our survey (69%) felt that HM Treasury only considered the impact of spending decisions over the spending review period, and not beyond (paragraph 4.4).

Principle 4

An understanding of the capability to deliver

Realism about what is required to transform services, ideally based on past experience, is essential. It is critical that departments and their partners have both the skills and capacity to make the changes.

Our 2012 report, *Managing budgeting in government*, found that "Spending teams considered that they have the capacity and capability to provide sufficient challenge. However, staff churn is a significant risk to knowledge retention."

18 HM Treasury, departments, and experts across government could have worked together better to assess whether plans are feasible or departments are capable of carrying them out. Expert stakeholders assessed departments' plans in some cases where the plans involved significant change. In some cases, such as the Government Property Unit, this was a systematic exercise. However, in other cases this was not done consistently and it is unclear how experts' advice was acted on. The value of expert engagement was also limited by the length of time they had during the Spending Review to examine plans (paragraphs 5.2 to 5.4).

19 The short timetable of the spending review places heavy demands on the capacity of both HM Treasury and departments. Just over half of finance directors who responded to our survey felt that HM Treasury had sufficient capability to challenge their complete submissions robustly and in detail. All the other respondents felt that HM Treasury could challenge at least some of their submissions robustly. Departments themselves were able to provide differing levels of resource during the Spending Review process which did not necessarily reflect the complexity of their plans (paragraphs 5.5 to 5.8).

Principle 5

Timely information on performance to review success and hold departments to account

A critical aspect of ensuring that projects are delivered successfully is maintaining an understanding of how they are performing. Relevant and timely information needs to be available to decision-makers.

Our 2012 report, *Managing budgeting in government,* noted that "Departments vary in the extent to which finance and performance reporting are brought together and any performance indicators are often milestones and deliverables rather than outcomes."

20 The spending review remains focused on finances. HM Treasury and Cabinet Office are working to improve the link between financial management and performance, but the pace of this has been slow. We (and the Committee of Public Accounts) have commented repeatedly on past failures to adequately link financial and performance information. Settlement letters do not set out detail on how departments will monitor performance, alongside the detail on how they will allocate funding to policy objectives (paragraphs 6.2 and 6.3).

21 Single departmental plans, announced alongside the Spending Review, are meant to strengthen the link between financial management and performance by requiring departments to set out how their spending review settlements link to their planned objectives and actions. The plans are still being developed, and HM Treasury is working alongside Cabinet Office to develop connections, which both departments and spending teams find valuable. This work is covered in more detail in our report on the single departmental plans (paragraphs 6.6 to 6.9).[7]

7 Comptroller and Auditor General, *Government's management of its performance: progress with Single Departmental Plans*, Session 2016-17, HC 872, National Audit Office, July 2017.

Conclusion on value for money

22 The spending review process sets clear limits on departmental spending. This allows departments to plan for the medium term and align policy priorities with their budgets. HM Treasury has made some positive changes to the spending review process, including improvements in how it works with departments and other parts of the centre of government, such as Cabinet Office. However, the process and supporting financial management system still do not make full use of the expertise within the centre of government, or incentivise collaboration across departments.

23 The way the spending review process works does not sufficiently address some fundamental issues with the way government functions. It also does not fully address previous concerns that we and the Committee of Public Accounts have raised. HM Treasury's approach remains rooted in bilateral negotiation. This allows it to function well as a control on departmental spending. However, it prevents the spending review from maximising the value for money of spending by tackling difficult and entrenched issues. These include both policy issues such as obesity and structural issues such as interdependencies between departments and the services they provide. Focusing on spending allocations and their consequences within just the spending review period reduces the attention paid to the longer term.

24 HM Treasury has made some progress in improving the spending review process, however it does not yet provide the best environment for achieving value for money. The spending review is undoubtedly a complex and difficult exercise. Improving the process and the wider engagement with departments would help HM Treasury to create a more mature planning and budgeting environment.

25 HM Treasury has asked us to record that it considers the spending review process is effective in prioritising resources and delivering value for money. It does not agree with a number of the NAO's key findings including in relation to joint working across departments, consulting with experts and longer term thinking.

Recommendations

a **HM Treasury should engage more openly with departments.** There has been a closer relationship between HM Treasury and finance staff in government departments. HM Treasury and the departments should seek to build on these relationships to build a less transactional spending review process. This would allow them to have better discussions about departments' ability to deliver their programmes and the necessary trade-offs between different policies and programmes.

b **HM Treasury should offer incentives for departments to work together and submit joint bids by introducing a system view to the spending review process rather than enforcing existing departmental boundaries.** HM Treasury should capitalise on departments' willingness to collaborate. It should make sure that the spending review process is not a barrier to aligning spending with cross-government commitments, such as the Cabinet-level implementation taskforces.

c **HM Treasury should develop a better understanding of where departments need to plan for longer periods and how to support this in the spending review.** This does not necessarily mean extending the period that settlements cover. It could also look at the impact of decisions taken for the next five years on future spending or future needs, or how uncertainty about the future may lead to changing spending requirements.

d **HM Treasury, departments and the finance profession should build on existing cross-departmental cooperation and continue to develop tools to better understand departmental spending.** As part of this, HM Treasury should ensure that it continues to engage with departments to understand their models and forecasts before formally launching a spending review.

e **The spending review should be an exercise led by HM Treasury's spending teams, but carried out by the whole centre of government.** HM Treasury should make more use of the expertise across the centre of government during the process, both to challenge and understand specific departmental plans, and to ensure consistency in dealing with common areas of spend.

f **HM Treasury and Cabinet Office should work with departments to link spending decisions to performance against outcomes.** HM Treasury should consider whether there is scope to improve settlement letters by asking departments for information about their plans to measure performance as well as spending. HM Treasury should also use the performance measures being developed as part of the single departmental plans to assess departmental progress during this spending review period.

g **Cabinet Office and HM Treasury should continue to work on achieving a seamless link between the single departmental plans as a tool for continuous business planning and performance management, and the periodic spending reviews as a high-level "reboot" exercise to respond to changes in administration, fiscal readjustments or other fundamental shifts.** They set out to integrate the Spending Review 2015 and single departmental plans but in practice this was too ambitious to achieve in one year. Doing so will enhance the quality of spending review decisions and serve to embed the single departmental plan approach for the long term.

Part One

Importance of spending reviews

The aims and purpose of spending reviews

1.1 Spending reviews are led by HM Treasury, and set multi-year budgets for departments in line with the government's policy priorities.[8] Their format has changed since they were introduced in 1998. Spending reviews now do more to consider the government's aggregate spending in the wider context of taxation and fiscal sustainability. Since 2010, spending reviews have focused on making spending cuts, but their main purpose – allocating budgets – has not changed (**Figure 2**).

1.2 Spending reviews help to set government priorities and allocate high-level departmental budgets. Over the course of a spending review period, other formal fiscal events such as Budgets allow the government to make changes to departmental spending plans if necessary. As spending review settlements are published in summary form, they are also a useful tool for public accountability. They provide Parliament with information on funding that it can set against outcomes. The settlements also provide the parameters within which departments carry out their own more detailed planning.

1.3 Spending reviews clearly set out medium-term spending. This is demonstrated by the close correlation between the changes in total spending set out in a spending review and actual spend (**Figure 3** on page 22). Over the 2010 and 2013 spending review periods, departments lowered their overall spending to meet the agreed spending controls (**Figure 4** on page 23). Minor changes made in other fiscal events, such as Budgets, show that settlements are flexible.

1.4 The spending review exercise is a complex and resource-intensive effort for HM Treasury. The Organisation for Economic Cooperation and Development (OECD) commended the UK spending review system for covering the whole of government spending after its scope was expanded from 2010 onwards.[9]

8 Comptroller and Auditor General, *Managing budgeting in government*, Session 2012-13, HC 597, National Audit Office, October 2012, paragraph 1.7.

9 Organisation for Economic Cooperation and Development, *Working Party of Senior Budget Officials, Performance budgeting practices and procedures: case studies*, Eleventh Annual Meeting of the Organisation for Economic Cooperation and Development Senior Budget Officials Performance and Results Network, November 2015.

Figure 2
Spending review process

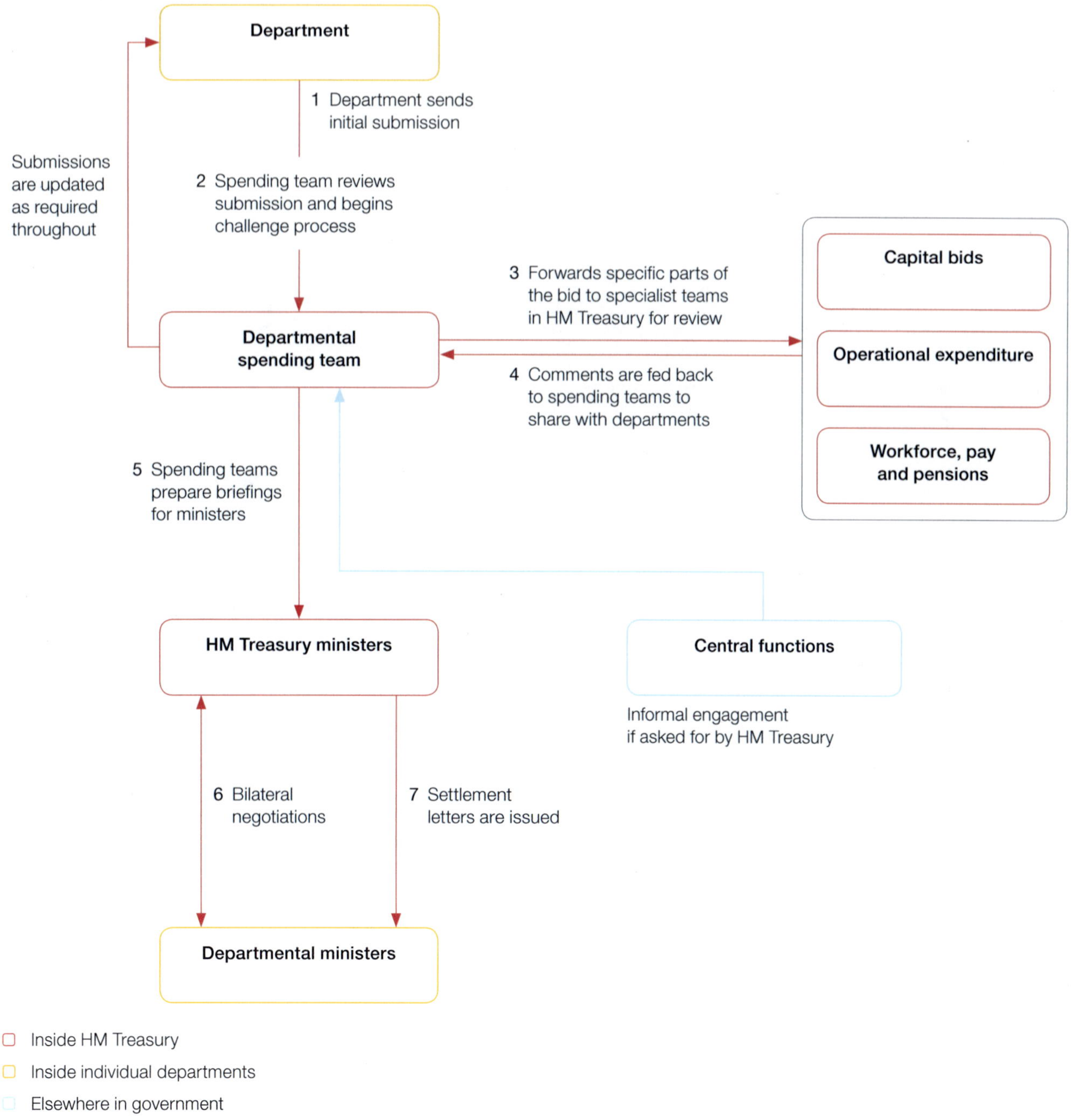

Source: National Audit Office analysis of HM Treasury information

Figure 3

Growth in spending in successive spending reviews: comparison of plans and spend

The changes in spending set out in spending reviews are closely matched by what departments then actually spent

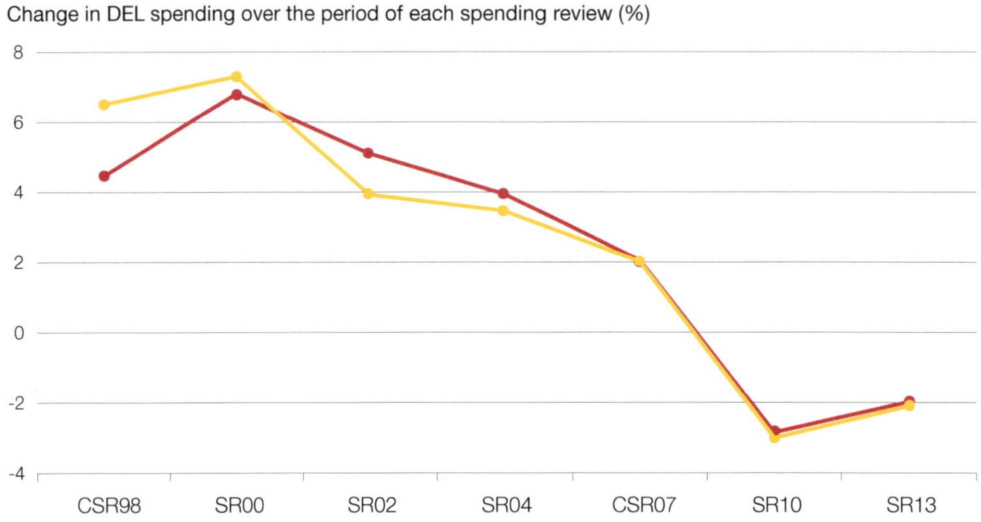

	CSR98	SR00	SR02	SR04	CSR07	SR10	SR13
● DEL plans							
● DEL outturn	6.52	7.31	3.93	3.47	2.02	-2.99	-2.10

Note

1 CSR = Comprehensive Spending Review; SR = Spending Review/Round; DEL = Departmental Expenditure Limits (comprising resource and capital).

Source: National Audit Office analysis of published HM Treasury data

Wider financial management

1.5 Alongside the Spending Review 2013, HM Treasury published a Financial Management Review. This aimed to improve the tools and techniques available for it to make good decisions during subsequent reviews. The aim was for HM Treasury and departments to:

a "better understand the costs of activities and ensure this understanding will be used to better inform decision-making;

b define standards for costing and management information; and

c accelerate current initiatives required to support a common framework, including adopting the common chart of accounts."[10]

10 HM Treasury, *Review of financial management in government*, December 2013.

Figure 4

Department for Work & Pensions' 2010 Spending Review settlement compared with outturn spending, 2011-12 to 2015-16

Actual spending by the Department lowered in line with the budget set at the Spending Review

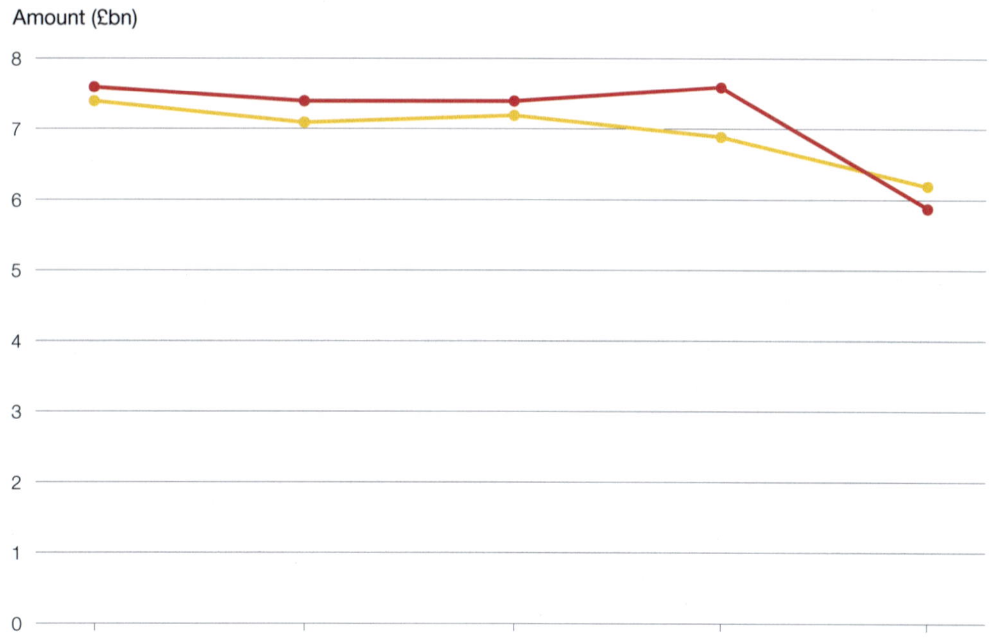

	2011-12	2012-13	2013-14	2014-15	2015-16
● 2010 Spending Review settlement	7.6	7.4	7.4	7.6	5.9
● Outturn	7.4	7.1	7.2	6.9	6.2

Note

1 Resource Departmental Expenditure Limits (RDEL): the budget allocated to departments for resource spending (eg administration costs and day-to-day running of services).

Source: National Audit Office analysis of published HM Treasury data

Spending Review 2015

1.6 In the Spending Review 2015 announcement, the government stated that it would use the review to "set out plans for eliminating the deficit and safeguarding Britain's long-term economic security", intending for the Spending Review to act as a strong control on spending.[11] The government also saw the Spending Review as an opportunity to "invest in its priorities, and deliver ambitious reforms to modernise and localise public services to achieve better outcomes for citizens".

11 From HM Treasury, *A country that lives within its means: Spending Review 2015*, Cm 9112, July 2015, available at: www.gov.uk/government/uploads/system/uploads/attachment_data/file/447101/a_country_that_lives_within_its_means.pdf

1.7 The Spending Review 2015 process formally started on 21 July 2015. HM Treasury sent out requests for departmental submissions and published a summary document setting out their plans. HM Treasury's formal request asked departments to submit two scenarios: a 25% and 40% reduction in spending. HM Treasury expected submissions by 4 September 2015, just seven weeks later. The Spending Review was published on 25 November 2015, 11 weeks after submissions were due (**Figure 5**).[12]

Figure 5
Spending Review timeline

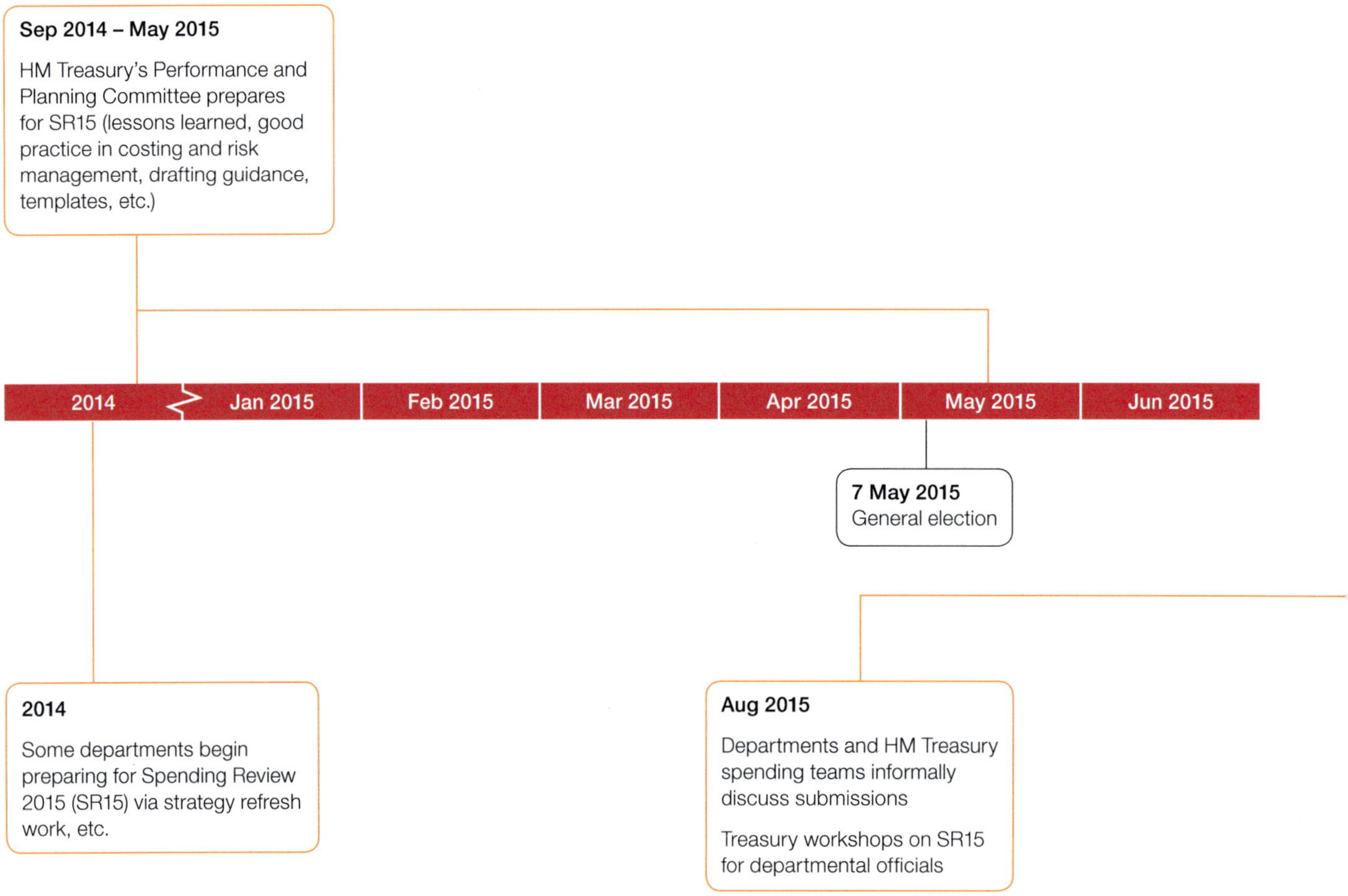

Source: National Audit Office analysis of HM Treasury data

12 HM Treasury, *Spending Review and Autumn Statement 2015*, Cm 9162, November 2015, available at: www.gov.uk/government/publications/spending-review-and-autumn-statement-2015-documents

1.8 The Spending Review honoured previous commitments to 'protect' the spending of certain departments over the Parliament. The Chancellor had also set a target to achieve a budget surplus by the end of 2019-20. The Spending Review announced reductions in the resource spending of 'unprotected' departments of £21.5 billion by 2019-20, of which £9.5 billion would be reinvested. Overall departmental spending was planned to reduce by 2.1% (£7.4 billion) in real terms.

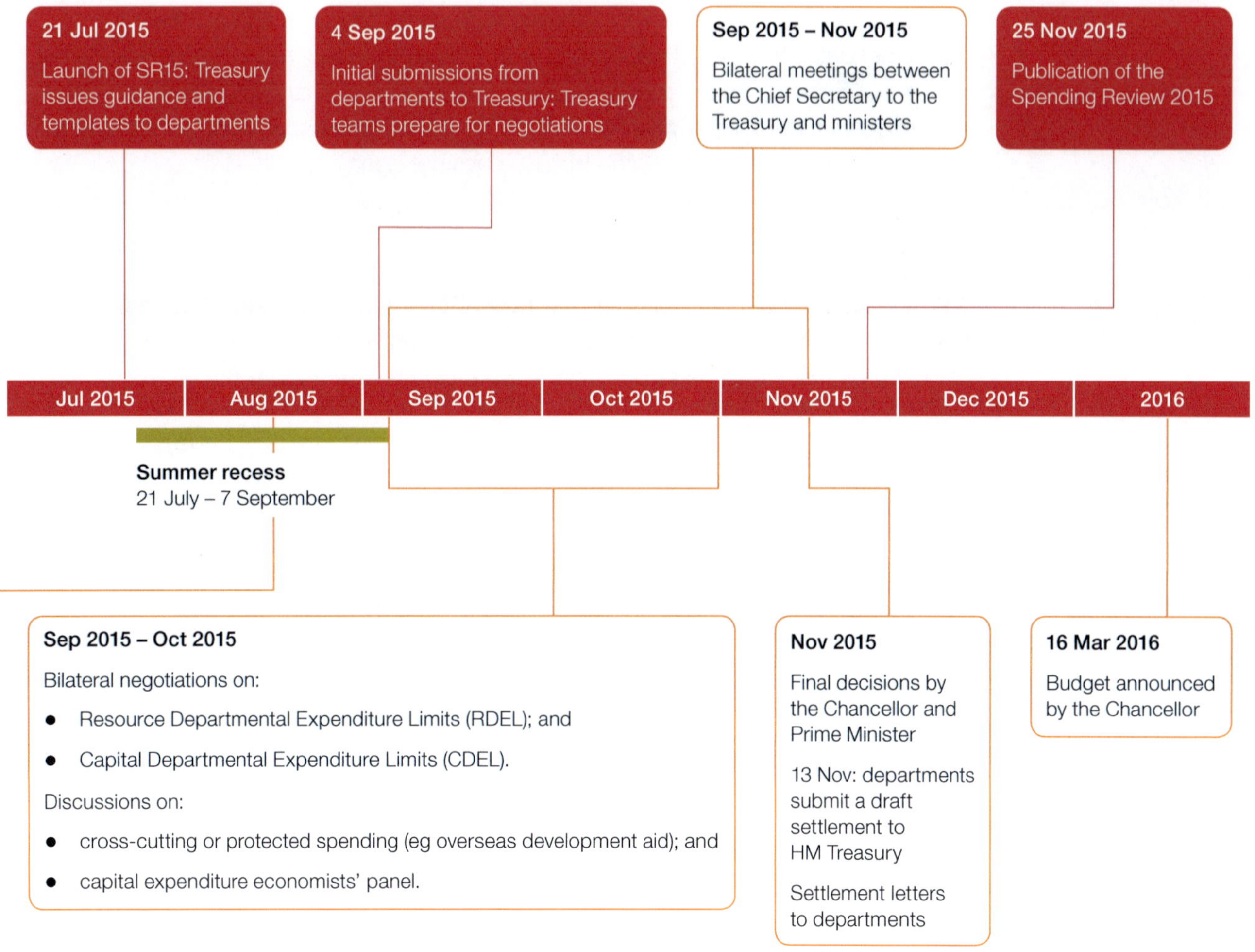

Our previous work

1.9 The government does not have a strong track record in robust longer-term business planning. A large number of our reports have identified common issues that lead to poor implementation of government programmes. They also found that past spending reviews have been characterised by a short-term approach. Our 2012 report on managing budgeting found that the data required to inform decisions on allocating spending were not readily available (especially on resource spending).[13] It also commented that the budget system lacked clear links to results and was insufficiently integrated with business. It also did not encourage collaboration between departments.

1.10 HM Treasury and departments have made some progress against the recommendations in the 2013 Committee of Public Accounts' report (Appendix Three).[14] However, progress has been incremental, and the pace of change has been slower than expected, particularly in areas such as cross-government working, where some promising developments we noted in 2012 have not been capitalised on.

Principles for making good budgeting decisions

1.11 We have set out principles for making well-informed budgeting decisions. In summer 2015, based on insights from our previous work, we developed a series of principles that would underpin a 'good' spending review (**Figure 6**).

13 Comptroller and Auditor General, *Managing budgeting in government*, Session 2012-13, HC 597, National Audit Office, October 2012.

14 HC Committee of Public Accounts, *Managing budgeting in government*, Thirty-fourth Report of Session 2012-13, HC 661, February 2013.

Figure 6
Principles for making well-informed decisions

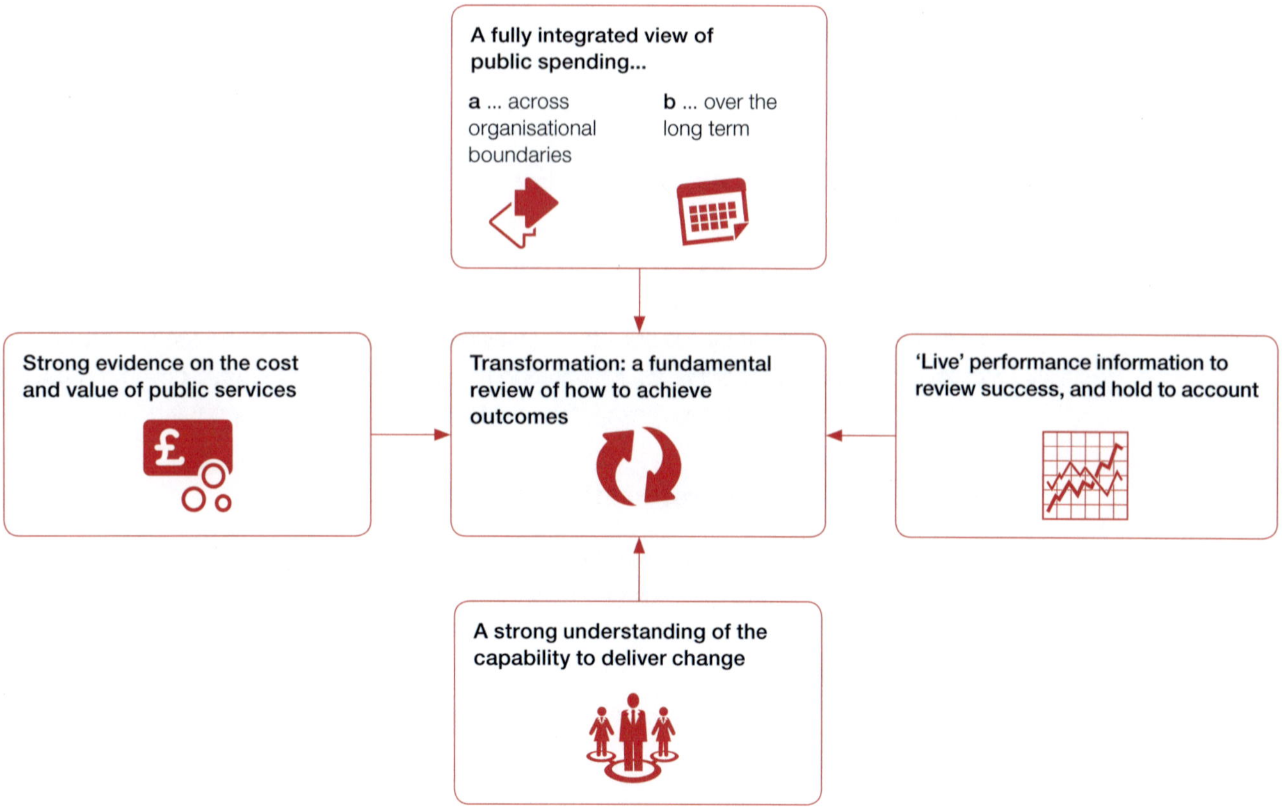

Source: National Audit Office analysis

Part Two

Evidence to support decisions

2.1 Robust evidence is essential to ensure that decisions made during a spending review are defensible. HM Treasury and departments need to work together to understand whether they are currently achieving value for money, and the drivers of costs and demand for services. Information must be consistent across programmes and across departments, to make fair comparisons and prioritise spending.

Spending Review preparation

2.2 Before the Spending Review 2015 began, HM Treasury took steps to understand the evidence base that underpinned departmental forecasts and baseline models. These preparations ranged from 'teach-ins' (eg on departmental programmes) to the early submission of evidence to explain assumptions and figures. This helped HM Treasury teams develop a good understanding of departments' business.

2.3 All four of our case study departments began preparing their evidence base between six and 18 months before the formal launch. They reported some engagement with HM Treasury during this period (Figure 5). However, there was no formal process for HM Treasury spending teams to discuss the models and forecasts that would underpin spending review submissions with their departments.

2.4 HM Treasury also explained processes to staff in departments before the formal announcement. It set out what would happen during the Spending Review, and what evidence departments should develop and provide. It carried out substantial engagement with finance directors across government, using cross-departmental committees set up as part of the Financial Management Review. In particular, the Planning and Performance Committee was involved in spending review plans from February 2015.

2.5 Once the formal spending review process began, the preparations already carried out allowed HM Treasury's spending teams and departments to focus more on specific spending decisions, since forecasts and baselines had already been shared (**Figure 7**). The case study departments thought that developing good relationships with their spending teams at HM Treasury was essential to achieving a successful settlement. This included providing HM Treasury with robust evidence to support their bids.

Figure 7

Evidence-sharing between departments and HM Treasury

Case study departments felt it was important to ensure that HM Treasury's spending teams could understand the interactions between capital, administration and programme costs and Annual Managed Expenditure well enough to realise the consequences that spending decisions in one part of the business might have on another. Examples include: understanding the resource implications of large capital budgets to mitigate against the risk of signing up to large infrastructure projects without having the necessary resources to manage them; and the effect that cutting front-line services such as jobcentres would have on the forecast number of people remaining on benefits rather than moving into work.

It was essential for departments going through major transformational change to explain the reasons for, and importance of, their spending patterns. Examples included: investment in infrastructure that could lead to savings in running costs; or the importance of a new IT system to support transformation plans. It was also important for departments to make clear where small areas of expenditure were critical to achieving a manifesto commitment or at the heart of a transformation programme and should not be discounted by spending teams as unimportant.

Department for Transport

The Department for Transport's (DfT) strategy for the Spending Review 2015 was to provide good evidence for the funds it needed, and to engage with HM Treasury, staff, ministers, stakeholders and other government departments. DfT started preparing for the Spending Review in January 2014 in stages, including:

1 the policies it wanted to achieve;

2 the environment within which policies need to be delivered; and

3 options for delivering the elected government's policies.

DfT's spending team at HM Treasury welcomed early discussions, but DfT's early engagement with other government departments was limited, since potential partner departments were working to different timescales in preparing for the Spending Review. During the spending review process, departments were not openly discussing their bid submissions with each other.

Source: National Audit Office

Financial management tools

2.6 A key part of HM Treasury's plans for implementing the Financial Management Review was to develop evidence-based tools, particularly to help with costing and understanding the value of service delivery. These would help to inform spending reviews. In our report *The centre of government: an update*, published in March 2015, we said:[15]

> "The next major test for financial management implementation will be the impact on planning, agreeing and implementing the spending review. Many of the actions under way would provide valuable support for spending review discussions if there are comparable results for all departments. In particular, those actions which aim to provide deeper understanding of the drivers of costs, and those which try to present a complete picture of departmental risks. The current plan is for key tools to be rolled out to all departments in 2015, in time for a possible spending review in autumn."

15 Comptroller and Auditor General, *The centre of government: an update*, Session 2014-15, HC 1031, National Audit Office, March 2015.

2.7 HM Treasury and departments did not deliver these tools within the intended timescale. HM Treasury made available early versions of tools to look at unit costs, and to assess the relative value and riskiness of programmes. But the information was not robust enough to inform the Spending Review 2015, and the tools were not detailed enough and not completed consistently across departments.

2.8 HM Treasury received limited evidence from departments on wider issues, such as the relative value for money of programmes. We noted the same issue in our 2012 report, in which we said that "The data required to inform decision-makers on optimal resource allocation was not readily available and in some places did not exist".[16] HM Treasury asked departments to provide information on the relative value of their programmes. Of the four formal submissions we reviewed, only one had done this. Some 10 of the 14 finance directors who responded to our survey said they completed the value-for-money assessment for either some or none of their programmes (**Figure 8**).

2.9 Some aspects of the Financial Management Review did support the spending review process. The Planning and Performance committee had a role in spending review preparation, interacting with finance teams in departments. The Committee produced a lessons learned document based on previous spending reviews, and provided input into guidance and workshops. HM Treasury has told us it intends to carry out more work in the future, and announced at the Spending Review that a dedicated Costing Unit would be set up to help departments in the future.

Figure 8
Summary of survey findings on evidence to support decisions

Question	Summary of responses
In 2013, as part of the Financial Management Review (FMR), HM Treasury set up work streams to improve financial management in government: how much did the following work streams contribute to improvements ahead of the Spending Review 2015?	A roughly equal proportion of respondents agreed that the FMR strands had not contributed to improvements, or that some insights were applied to the Spending Review 2015. Only two respondents thought the people and performance and planning strand and the people strand had generated crucial insights for the Spending Review 2015. Six departments left comments: four noted that the work was not mature enough to take advantage of during the Spending Review 2015, or that it had not made much difference. Three noted that the FMR has generated good outputs and products, some of which were taken forward to inform policy and operational choices, or that the department had a financial improvement plan based on the FMR.
When preparing its submission for the Spending Review 2015, did your department make use of the relative value-for-money (VfM) assessment section of the submission template?	Responses were mixed, with four departments reporting that they did not use relative VFM assessments; six mentioning they had used it for some programmes; and four saying they had used it for all programmes. Six respondents left comments: four were negative, saying either that they made limited use of VFM assessments, arguing that the format of the data required was too simplistic to inform decision-making, or mentioning that the department had used relative VFM assessments, but they had not been helpful. Four mixed comments noted that some departments were taking some of this approach forward through value maps or in other ways.

Source: National Audit Office survey of finance directors

16 Comptroller and Auditor General, *Managing budgeting in government*, Session 2012-13, HC 597, National Audit Office, October 2012.

Wider evidence

2.10 HM Treasury did some specific work to target key areas, which supported its decision-making:

- **Capital spending**

  In line with the exercises carried out in 2010 and 2013, a central team of experts reviewed all capital projects together. HM Treasury required departments to provide consistent information on their projects, such as funding required by year, net present value of the project, and whether the project had been awarded funding in 2013, as well as more detailed supporting bids. A cross-government panel of experts reviewed the information and made recommendations. While we believe this exercise had some weaknesses, particularly in linking information on capital spend to revenue plans, this cross-governmental focus is valuable.

- **Pay and workforce**

  A central team in HM Treasury collected standard information on pay, headcount, pay awards and recruitment and retention as part of the submission template that all departments were asked to complete. Rather than making specific recommendations as the capital panel did, this team provided feedback on departments' proposals which fed into the overall work carried out by departmental spending teams, and then translated into recommendations for ministers.

- **Operational expenditure**

  HM Treasury also asked departments to provide consistent information on operational areas of spend such as ICT, estates and consultants. However, the departments did not provide as much detail about this expenditure, hampering meaningful comparisons. HM Treasury is building on its experience of the Spending Review 2015 to align categories of spend with the aim of having more information for future fiscal events.

Part Three

An integrated view across organisational boundaries

3.1 The government is increasingly tackling complex policy areas that sit outside the boundaries of single departments. A spending review must encourage departments to work together to achieve cross-departmental outcomes. Many government services already work together, which means spending decisions in one area may have knock-on effects on demand in others. HM Treasury and departments must understand these links to maximise value for money.

Cross-departmental working and joint bids

3.2 HM Treasury acknowledged our recommendation on the Spending Review 2010 that Treasury spending teams should foster collaboration. Its guidance to departments recommends that they deliver joint bids where a government objective depends on more than one department:

> "Cross-cutting spending
>
> 26. Where a government objective depends on more than one department, departments should work closely together to deliver it in the most cost effective manner.
>
> 27. To submit a joint bid, departments should produce a single submission for the policy objective, including details of the elements of their baselines currently spent on it. Departments should be clear in their returns how funding for joint bids is split between contributing departments.
>
> 28. The Treasury also encourages departments to include joint or complementary performance objectives setting out what they intend to achieve for the money spent. Departments should provide SR submissions covering their residual baselines. Where departments wish to provide joint submissions they should agree this with their Treasury spending teams."[17]

17 Quote from guidance issued to departments at the start of the 2015 Spending Review process.

3.3 However, there has been little progress since our 2012 report, which noted that "the budgetary system does not incentivise departments to collaborate".[18] HM Treasury's submission process remains set up along individual departmental lines, which does not encourage cross-departmental working. Its submission template set no explicit requirements for departments to commit to joint working although it was suggested in the guidance. Departments were working together informally, but HM Treasury received only two formal joint bids across all departmental submissions, which was the same number as in 2010. Case study departments commented that the bilateral nature of the process may not produce the best outcomes for resourcing across the whole of government.

3.4 Some HM Treasury departmental spending teams are grouped together and share leads, for example the Energy, Environment and Agriculture team covers both the Department of Energy & Climate Change (DECC) and the Department for Environment, Food & Rural Affairs (**Figure 9** overleaf). However, many current cross-government priorities do not align with HM Treasury's spending team structure. HM Treasury relies on its own management structures, such as establishing specific boards to address cross-cutting issues, to maintain oversight of the complex interdependencies between different areas of spending.

3.5 HM Treasury could use existing systems to support more joint budgeting across themes and issues. For example, the government has established 11 Cabinet-level implementation taskforces.[19] These all have remits that cut across departments, designed specifically to look at complex policy issues that involve multiple government departments. Not all taskforces cover issues with significant spending implications, for example the taskforce on Syrian returners. Some of the issues that specific taskforces deal with have more significant spending implications, but these were only partially considered at a cross-departmental level (**Figure 10** on page 35).

Examples of cross-government working

3.6 A wide range of activities went on informally to facilitate joint discussions between departments (**Figure 11** on page 36). Discussions and roundtables were held between ministers on cross-cutting policies such as devolution and overseas development aid prior to departments submitting their returns. Departments worked with each other at a more thematic level outside the formal spending review process; for example:

- special teams were set up for joint working, featuring joint governance arrangements, although funding remained separate (Figure 11); and
- departments agreed common assumptions for areas of work which overlapped, so that bids prepared by different departments were consistent.

18 Comptroller and Auditor General, *Managing budgeting in government*, Session 2012-13, HC 597, National Audit Office, October 2012, paragraph 17.

19 These are: Childcare; Child Protection; Digital Infrastructure and Inclusion; Earn or Learn; Exports; Health and Social Care; Housing; Immigration; Syrian Returners; Tackling extremism in communities; and Troubled Families.

Figure 9
Size of spending teams

Group	Total staff in each team
Public Service Group	118
Enterprise and Growth Unit	60
Personal Tax, Welfare and Pensions	52
Public Spending Group	25
International and Europe Group	6
Fiscal Group	1
Total	**262**

Source: National Audit Office analysis of HM Treasury information

Figure 10

Mapping the Housing Taskforce to departments

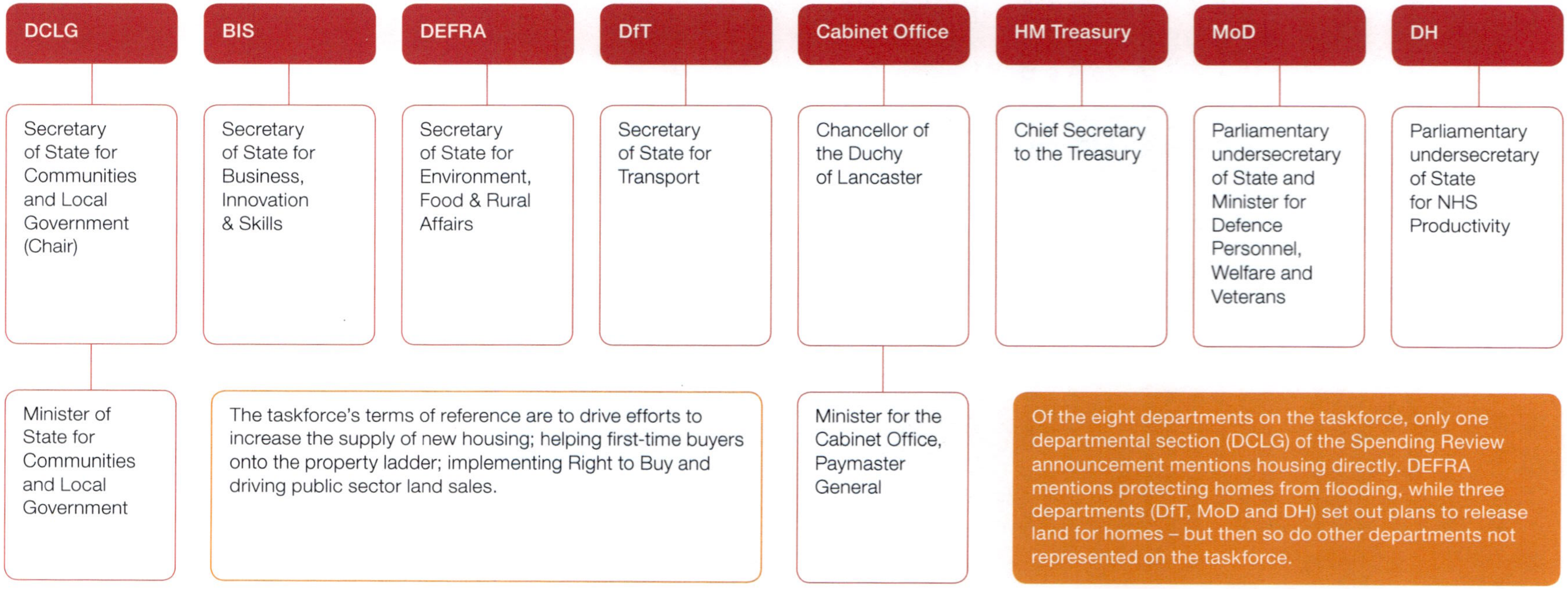

Note

1 DCLG = Department for Communities and Local Government, BIS = Department for Business, Innovation & Skills, DEFRA = Department for Environment, Food & Rural Affairs, DfT = Department for Transport, MoD = Ministry of Defence, DH = Department of Health.

Source: National Audit Office analysis of HM Treasury information

Figure 11

Examples of cross-government working

Joint working arrangements

The Department for Education (DfE) and Department for Business, Innovation & Skills (BIS) both have policy responsibility for apprenticeships – DfE for 16 to 18 years old and BIS for 19+ years. Although they worked together, the departments told us that in the past their arrangements had not felt very joined-up. Consequently, they held a number of discussions before the start of the Spending Review to develop closer working arrangements.

Following the General Election, the government raised the profile of the apprenticeships agenda. One of the government's key manifesto commitments was to create 3 million extra apprenticeship places over the life of the current Parliament. In July 2015, DfE, BIS and the Skills Funding Agency (SFA) created a joint group known as the 16+ Skills Portfolio, which includes the Joint Apprenticeships Unit. It reports to one minister, and has a joint secretariat and senior responsible officers from all three organisations. BIS and DfE have joint responsibility for three programmes run by the unit, while BIS, SFA and DfE have joint responsibility for another.

Early feedback from DfE is that the unit is working well. Teams have had to overcome different styles of working and different cultures to be effective, but the unit is able to work at a faster pace and in a more informed manner than when the teams worked separately. This reduces the number of monthly meetings required to keep colleagues informed of progress or decisions made in other teams. There are fewer gaps in the combined team's knowledge and it is better able to accommodate the priorities and pressures of both departments.

Common assumptions

The Department for Work & Pensions (DWP) and HM Revenue & Customs (HMRC) worked together to agree common assumptions on the number of people moving to Universal Credit. These fed into both departments' spending review submissions.

People receiving Universal Credit no longer separately receive tax credits administered by HMRC, such as Child Tax Credit and Working Tax Credit. This reduces HMRC's workload, and increases the workload in DWP. The two departments worked together before submitting their spending review bids to ensure that the models for future workload in both departments were based on a common set of assumptions of the number of people moving onto Universal Credit, and therefore off the tax credits administered by HMRC.

Source: National Audit Office

3.7 HM Treasury could expand its role in facilitating good practice and ensuring that common policy areas are agreed between departments. All finance directors who responded said that the Treasury at least partially encouraged them to consider cross-departmental issues, although the majority told us they received no support or guidance from HM Treasury to do this (**Figure 12**). We found examples where informal working arrangements broke down because preparations in different departments developed at different times, or departments could not agree common policy objectives (**Figure 13**). While it is essential that departments collaborate informally to achieve the government's outcomes, without the structure of a formal joint bid there may be limits to the accountability of such arrangements. Where informal arrangements are unsuccessful, it will be more difficult for the government to identify areas where departments need to collaborate.

Figure 12

Summary of survey findings on cross-government working

Question	Summary of responses
Did HM Treasury encourage your department to consider cross-departmental issues in your submission?	Nine respondents said HM Treasury partially encouraged consideration of cross-departmental issues in submissions but provided no support; four said they did encourage consideration of cross-departmental issues and provided support. Seven departments left comments: two mentioned that HM Treasury encouraged engagement with other department(s); two mentioned that the spending review framework does not encourage departments to consider cross-departmental issues. Two mentioned that there was insufficient guidance on what was expected (and that input and guidance from Cabinet Office on issues such as digital transformation was limited). One mentioned that HM Treasury could have told them which issues in other departments would have affected them.
When preparing your submission, did your department coordinate with other departments on cross-departmental issues?	Thirteen respondents mentioned that they had either coordinated with other departments on cross-departmental issues or coordinated with other departments and shared the results with HM Treasury. Six respondents left comments about collaboration efforts ranging from joint working units to coordinating elements of spending review submissions. Two comments mentioned that time pressures made it difficult to engage with other departments, and that little progress had been made on other generic cross-departmental work.
From your perspective, how well did HM Treasury manage and coordinate the Spending Review 2015 (eg timeliness, communications and engagement with departments)?	Nine respondents thought HM Treasury managed some aspects of the Spending Review well, but not others; three thought that on the whole, it had managed the Spending Review well. Twelve respondents left comments: four were positive, highlighting good and timely communications, notably from spending teams. Six mixed comments mentioned that the overall timetable was right, but there was an issue with bids being requested shortly after the recess period; issues with short deadlines; and that the final stages of the process were unclear (with the capital process being seen as a 'black box'). The two negative comments focused on issues to do with short timelines, and the late/ad hoc treatment of capital.

Source: National Audit Office survey of finance directors

Figure 13

Circumstances that prevent joint bidding

The feedback we received from departments suggested that several of them could see the benefits of joint working and a number had attempted to work together. However, the negotiations failed during the spending review process for reasons such as: disagreements between ministers; disagreements about who should fund policy areas; and insufficient flexibility within single departmental plans to enable departments to work together:

- **Disagreements between ministers**
  Departments work to ministers' directions and a number of departments told us that it is not possible to arrange joint funding arrangements where ministers do not agree a way forward. In circumstances such as these there is currently no mechanism in the centre of government to find a solution.
- **Disagreements on funding responsibility**
  Departments are responsible for delivering projects within their policy areas. Sometimes these projects tackle part of an objective. We noted instances where departments with joint responsibility for a particular policy objective may have chosen to reallocate funding to meet other priorities. As a result, the department had a funding gap for the area of joint working. In these circumstances, the department with funding in place may be unwilling to fund the area that was supposed to be funded by the other department.
- **Insufficient flexibility within single departmental plans to enable departments to work together**
  The government recently introduced single departmental plans to merge various planning documents into one. Feedback from some departments noted the difficulty in reflecting joint arrangements within the plans.

The spending review process typically lasts for three months. Consequently, it is a high-pressure process. This may not be conducive to setting up joint working arrangements, which can be hard to get right to suit all the parties involved. In contrast, arrangements that are formed as part of business as usual, where the organisations involved have had time to establish the governance structures that work for them, are more likely to lead to sustainable solutions for the longer term.

Source: National Audit Office

Part Four

Taking a long-term view

4.1 The government recognises that much of the transformation it wishes to achieve cannot happen in a single spending review period. Decisions about spending and service provision should also be considered over the long term. This ensures that projects can run as expected and that long-term projects that can maximise value for money are not penalised due to short-term cut-offs.

4.2 The Spending Review is set up to focus on the projects and priorities that can be delivered during the period it covers. As we said in our previous report, "current budgetary processes cover the short and medium term. However, public services often have spending implications well beyond a four-year horizon".[20] HM Treasury must ensure that it understands these implications, so that the decisions it takes in the short term do not have serious unexpected long-term consequences.

4.3 HM Treasury has engaged informally with departments on longer-term projects. For example, its settlement with the Department for Transport (DfT) recognises that there will be successive road investment strategies that span the Spending Review 2015 period and beyond. In addition, the Spending Review recognises HM Treasury's commitments to 30-year funding streams for combined authorities that are subject to devolution deals, for investment in economic growth.

4.4 However, there is more to be done. Nine out of 13 finance directors felt that HM Treasury only considered the impact of spending decisions over the Spending Review period and not beyond (**Figure 14**). Our briefing to the Environmental Audit Committee found some evidence of consideration of long-term environmental issues within individual elements of the Spending Review, but there was no central assessment of whether the best results for long-term sustainability had been achieved.[21]

20 Comptroller and Auditor General, *Managing budgeting in government*, Session 2012-13, HC 597, National Audit Office, October 2012, paragraph 1.20.

21 National Audit Office, *Sustainability in the spending review*, July 2016. Available at: www.nao.org.uk/report/sustainability-in-the-spending-review

Figure 14

Summary of survey findings on the long-term view of the Spending Review

Question	Summary of responses
In your experience of the Spending Review 2015, over what period does HM Treasury consider the impacts of funding when agreeing departmental settlements?	Nine respondents said that HM Treasury considers the impact of settlement funding only during the Spending Review period; four mentioned that HM Treasury considers the impact in the medium term (eg five to 10 years). Eight respondents made comments. Two reiterated that HM Treasury mainly focused on the Spending Review period to 2020. Six mentioned issues around longer-term funding, but not impacts; either that they had made longer-term commitments that HM Treasury was aware of (or had discussions about), or that HM Treasury had provided some funding to ensure that programmes would not suddenly stop in 2020-21.

Source: National Audit Office survey of finance directors

The capital review exercise

4.5 HM Treasury reviewed bids for capital expenditure as a separate process within the Spending Review 2015, taking a 'zero-based approach'. This was designed to allow HM Treasury to compare bids, and departments' evidence on their impacts, across government and prioritise available funding between departments. While this approach brings benefits, it does create the risk of an artificial disconnect between capital and revenue, particularly where there are strong interdependencies. It also may mean that capital projects are funded while departments do not have the internal support to carry them out. All of our case study departments reported having separate discussions with HM Treasury on capital and resource. HM Treasury agreed that this was an area where it would like better information and more time to explore these relations.

4.6 Reflecting the purpose of the Spending Review, the capital bids received by HM Treasury are strongly skewed towards projects that are to be delivered within the Spending Review period (**Figure 15** overleaf). Only 47 out of 458 (10%) capital bids indicated that they would likely need capital funding past 2020-21, of which 29 bids (6%) were quantified. About 70% of these projects fall within the remit of two departments, DfT and the Department of Energy & Climate Change (DECC) (**Figure 16** on page 41). HM Treasury's ranking mechanism disadvantages long-term capital projects as it uses total capital invested, rather than the discounted figure used in the net present value calculation, although this mechanism is not the only method that HM Treasury uses to assess capital bids.

Figure 15
Profile of capital bids in Spending Review 2015

Few bids set out funding requirements for the period after 2020-21

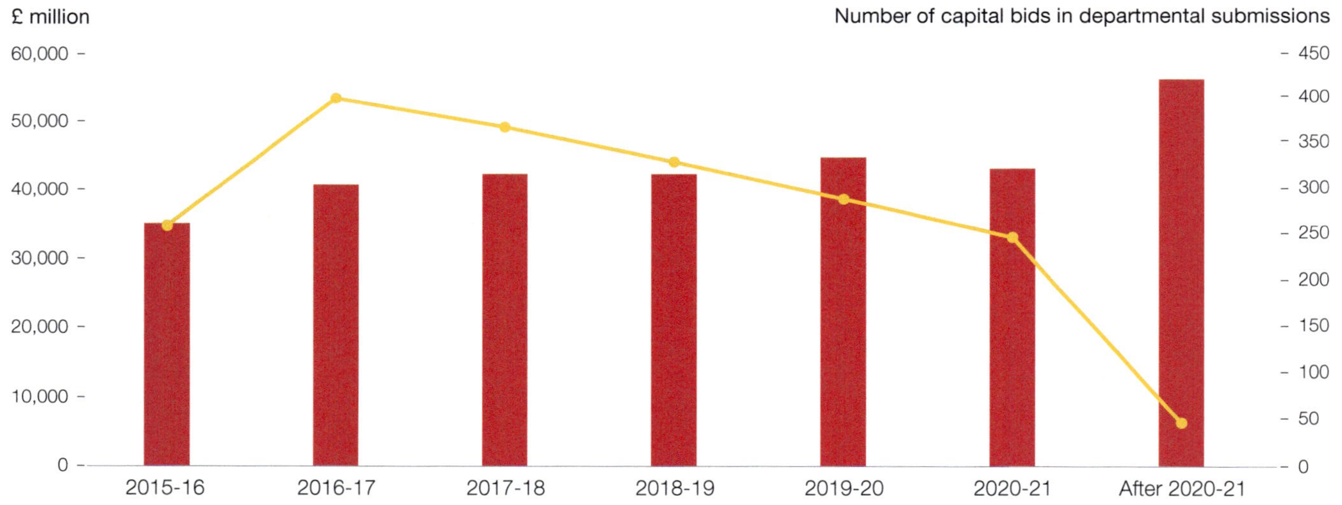

	2015-16	2016-17	2017-18	2018-19	2019-20	2020-21	After 2020-21
Total value of capital Departmental Expenditure Limit in bids	35,013	40,709	42,273	42,242	44,657	43,023	56,217
Number of bids with spend in year	260	400	368	330	289	247	47

Source: National Audit Office analysis of HM Treasury information

Figure 16

Number of projects with likely capital spending post 2020-21, by department

Seventy per cent of project spending capital past 2020-21 are within DfT and DECC

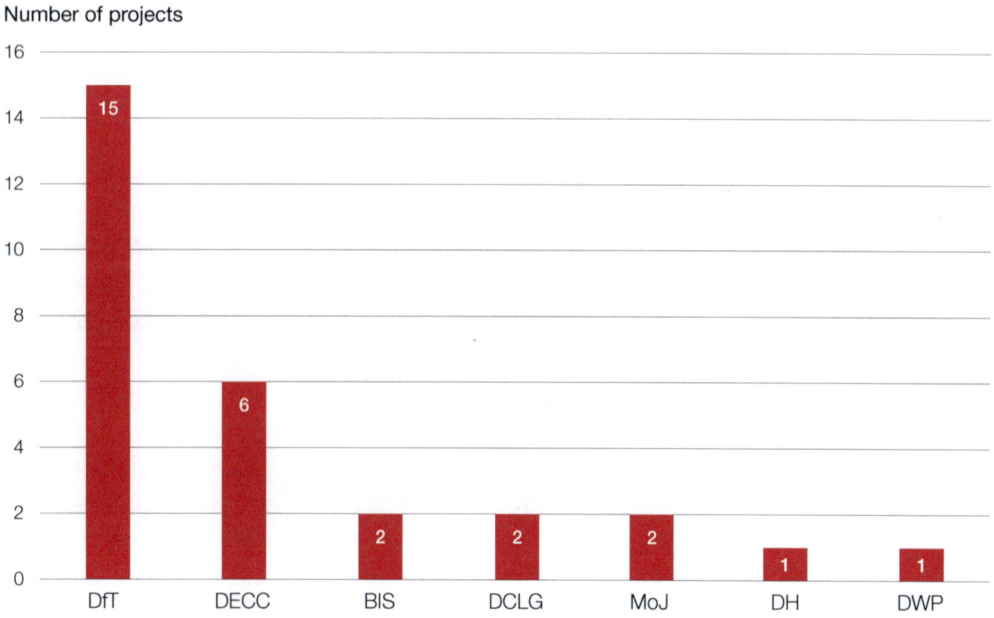

Note

1 DfT = Department for Transport; DECC = Department of Energy & Climate Change; BIS = Department for Business, Innovation & Skills; DCLG= Department for Communities and Local Government; MoJ = Ministry of Justice; DH = Department of Health; DWP = Department for Work & Pensions.

Source: National Audit Office analysis of HM Treasury information

4.7 This medium-term allocation of capital expenditure follows the progress made at the previous 2013 Spending Round, where 'capital-intensive' departments (such as Transport) were given six-year budgets for their core capital programmes – for example the Roads Investment Strategy. However, our work on project management suggests that there is still a bias towards projects that align with both the Spending Review period and the period of the Parliament (and therefore all stop and start at a similar time). Such a bias may hamper departments' ability to deliver a balanced portfolio of projects in the medium term.

Part Five

An understanding of the capability to deliver

5.1 Departments are increasingly trying to do more with less, and in many cases making substantial changes in how they deliver public services. This is difficult to achieve. It requires specialist expertise to assess the feasibility of any plans and to put individual plans in the context of change across the whole of government. It also requires an in-depth understanding of the plans and the specific challenges facing the departments.

Wider government expertise

5.2 When reviewing departmental submissions, HM Treasury's General Expenditure Policy team drew on the expertise of other teams internally, including on capital (paragraphs 2.9 and 4.5 to 4.7). The central team oversaw standard work across the submissions on capital spending, pay and workforce, and operational expenditure. This was designed to provide consistent information on the areas most likely to be affected by transformational change. HM Treasury's spending teams were then able to build this advice into their formal discussions with departments. However, with the exception of capital there was no formal process to ensure that this expert advice was included. HM Treasury intends to build on this to develop the capacity (and information) to do more detailed work on operational expenditure, and we expect it to look for other areas of spend that would benefit from such analysis.

5.3 Many departments' plans involved significant change – for example, moving services to digital provision or internal restructuring. Some individual departmental spending teams facilitated discussions between departments and experts across the centre of government, for example the Government Digital Service, the Crown Commercial Service or the Major Projects Authority (now the Infrastructure and Projects Authority). However, experts sometimes felt the value of their input was limited by the short amount of time they had to engage with the plans, and it is not clear whether these conversations had a significant influence on Spending Review outcomes. Our briefing for the Environmental Audit Committee also suggests that the government could make more use of experts in areas of sustainability, for example the Committee on Climate Change or the Natural Capital Committee.[22]

22 National Audit Office, *Sustainability in the spending review*, July 2016. Available at: www.nao.org.uk/report/sustainability-in-the-spending-review

5.4 This exercise will have most value if HM Treasury, departments, and the experts across government collaborate together and build up relationships which extend beyond the intensive spending review negotiations. There is evidence of HM Treasury engaging experts more systematically – for example on property (**Figure 17**). However, this was not always done consistently and it is unclear how expert advice was acted on.

Figure 17
Engagement with the Government Property Unit

HM Treasury asked the Government Property Unit (GPU), based in Cabinet Office, to carry out a review of departments' plans for moving out of offices. GPU has a detailed model of planned departmental moves, developed to support its own Spending Review submission and its subsequent work. It was able to use this to provide insight into departmental plans in a number of ways:

- reconciling the details of departments' plans with what GPU had modelled, to ensure that the forecast figures were accurate;
- providing a cross-departmental comparison of the ambition and maturity of departmental plans, so that the relevant spending teams could challenge departments that seemed to be either too optimistic in what they could achieve, or lacking in ambition; and
- providing standard phrasing to include commitments on property in departments' settlements.

Source: National Audit Office

Developing an in-depth understanding

5.5 HM Treasury needs to have the capability to understand whether departments are able to transform their operations. In our survey of finance directors, most departments reported favourably on their spending team's ability to challenge their submissions. However, a minority of departments commented unfavourably on levels of specialist knowledge, understanding of the department and capacity issues. Similarly, most case study departments thought its spending teams were well informed although a minority felt HM Treasury had capacity issues. Within the confines of the formal spending review process, HM Treasury can do little internally to alleviate these pressures, but it can look to external expertise to increase its capability.

5.6 HM Treasury's understanding will also depend on departments' ability to devote resources to the spending review process. Departments allocated varying levels of resources to prepare initial submissions and to interact with HM Treasury. Departments that were able to quantify the effort represented by the Spending Review 2015 mentioned arrangements ranging from staff carrying out spending review work in addition to their day jobs to a dedicated core team of 10 full-time staff.

5.7 The level of resources is not necessarily related to the complexity of a department's plans. This is important not only from the point of view of individual settlements, but also because settlements in one department can have a significant impact on others, and this also may not depend on their size.

5.8 Another key aspect of departments' capacity to deliver change is understanding their current position. Although there was no formal requirement from HM Treasury to do so, at least eight out 14 finance directors in our survey said that they mentioned previous cuts in spending as part of the context for their 2015 submissions. Some of our case study departments agreed departures from the standard submission of 25% and 40% spending reductions with HM Treasury on the basis of the reductions they had already made. Thirteen out of 14 said that HM Treasury considered the impact of previous cuts (**Figure 18**), although departments did not know to what extent this had an impact on decisions.

Figure 18
Summary of survey findings

Question	Summary of responses
Does your department record the resources (eg staff time, number of staff) committed to develop its submission for Spending Review 2015?	Most respondents (eight) said the department had no separate record of resources involved in preparing for Spending Review 2015. Eleven departments left comments: answers ranged from having no separate team, two to five staff for the core Spending Review team, to having nine to 10 full-time equivalent staff. Three respondents mentioned a specific time (six to 12 months) during which the team worked; five mentioned contributions from across the department besides the core team.
If previous reductions were included, did HM Treasury consider their impact as well as the consequences of reductions made for Spending Review 2015 (eg the cumulative impact of reductions) on your department?	Most respondents (13) mentioned that HM Treasury had considered the cumulative impact of reductions on some or all areas of the submission. Seven departments made comments: two mentioned how HM Treasury (including the spending team) had considered the cumulative impact on top of reductions delivered in the last Parliament.
In your experience of the Spending Review 2015, did HM Treasury have sufficient capability (eg staff, expertise, understanding of the department's business) to review and come up with suitable challenges to your department's submission?	All respondents mentioned that HM Treasury had sufficient capability to examine and challenge either some of the submission (six) or to issue robust and detailed challenge to the submission (seven). Six departments made comments: two were negative, and mentioned that the HM Treasury lead was overworked due to covering several departments, or that the HM Treasury team had limited capacity at times. Three mixed comments said the spending teams were good or understood the department but that some team members did not. They also pointed to gaps in areas such as ICT, and that the spending team's resources were often stretched.

Source: National Audit Office survey of finance directors

Part Six

Linking financial and performance information

6.1 In order to understand whether projects and programmes are being delivered successfully, the government must understand how a programme is performing. Timely feedback needs to be included in projects and be readily available to decision makers. The government can then capture performance data and link it to costs. This will provide a solid basis for future forecasts and spending decisions.

Work already in progress

6.2 We and the Committee of Public Accounts (the Committee) have repeatedly set out the need to link financial and performance information. In 2011, the Committee noted:

> "we expect sufficient information to enable us to hold departments to account on costs, outcomes and value for money on both the Coalition Agreement and across all of a department's work."[23]

6.3 Our 2012 report on budgeting recommended that HM Treasury should ask departments to set out the level of service they provide and how they will measure performance.[24] It also recommended that departments should ensure programme monitoring provides up-to-date data on services to inform decisions on allocating resources. Robust, up-to-date performance and cost data is one of the 'essentials of accountability' that we set out in our 2016 report.[25]

6.4 The Spending Review 2015 did little to set up expectations for the link between financial and performance information. We reviewed a sample of settlement letters, which had limited information on monitoring performance or allocating funding to policy objectives. The settlement letters did contain a standard paragraph on the need to evaluate impact robustly, in line with the principles of HM Treasury's guidance *Managing public money*. However, it is unclear how this will work in practice or what form the evaluation would take.

23 HC Committee of Public Accounts, *Departmental Business Planning*, Session 2010-12, HC 650, May 2011, p. 4.
24 Comptroller and Auditor General, *Managing budgeting in government*, Session 2012-13, HC 597, National Audit Office, October 2012.
25 Comptroller and Auditor General, *Accountability to Parliament for taxpayers' money*, Session 2015-16, HC 849, National Audit Office, February 2016.

6.5 Some departments recognise the need to present financial and performance information together. Some case study departments told us that they worked on integrating their Spending Review preparations with wider financial planning before the Spending Review 2015. This involved directorates collaborating to align performance and finance reporting.

6.6 In the past few years, HM Treasury and Cabinet Office have worked together to improve the link between financial management and performance, notably through the Financial Management Review. In 2015, the Planning and Performance Committee of finance directors across government worked on reporting, looking at international examples, and sought to continuously improve processes. At the same time, HM Treasury worked towards using accounts data to monitor efficiencies and identify opportunities to make savings by comparing departments' operational expenditure. This work is still in progress and was not widely used in the Spending Review 2015.

Single departmental plans

6.7 The government announced single departmental plans in July 2015 as a key counterpart to the Spending Review:[26]

> "... since SDPs are completely aligned with the Spending Review, they will enable us to bring together inputs (especially funding) with outputs – thus making clear the trade-offs and choices."

6.8 The published single departmental plans do not establish a clear link between funding and outcomes, and therefore fail to provide the public accountability we believe they should. The internal versions, which departments are sharing with Cabinet Office and HM Treasury, are more detailed. As these have not yet been finalised, it remains to be seen how strong the linkages are and how this information can be used in the future.

6.9 Our report *Government's management of its performance: progress with single departmental plans*, published alongside this one, recommends that the government do more to integrate the single departmental plans with future spending reviews, to contextualise submissions and settlements.[27] It also recommends that the spending review settlements and the single departmental plans should provide a consistent and agreed basis for discussions between Cabinet Office, HM Treasury and departments.

6.10 HM Treasury and Cabinet Office are moving towards greater integration to facilitate discussions with departments. It plans to use internal unpublished versions of the single departmental plans to support its engagement with departments. In particular, it expects that this will allow HM Treasury to have a more systematic approach to performance across government, and to look at future plans, not just past performance. It is not clear to what extent HM Treasury plans to use this information to make decisions on the basis of performance in the next spending review.

26 John Manzoni, 'Clarifying our priorities – Single Departmental Plans', 29 July 2015, available at: https://civilservice.blog.gov.uk/2015/07/29/clarifying-our-priorities-single-departmental-plans/

27 Comptroller and Auditor General, *Government's management of its performance: progress with Single Departmental Plans*, Session 2016-17, HC 872, National Audit Office, July 2017.

Appendix One

Our audit approach

1 This study examined whether the spending review is an effective mechanism for planning and allocating public money in the medium term. We reviewed:

- the importance of spending reviews;
- the extent to which the Spending Review 2015 addresses the key principles needed to make well-informed decisions; and
- the relationships that HM Treasury and departments have in place to achieve effective outcomes.

2 We applied an analytical framework with evaluative criteria. This included assessing the Spending Review against principles derived from our past work on what a 'good' spending review process would look like, which are aligned with national and international consensus. By 'good', we mean a process that is well integrated within wider financial management, and follows our principles for making well-informed decisions.

3 In examining the Spending Review, our work focuses on how the process enables sound, evidence-based decision-making, rather than the decisions themselves. We have not evaluated the quality of departmental bids.

4 Our audit approach is summarised in **Figure 19** overleaf. Our evidence base is described in Appendix Two.

Figure 19
Our audit approach

The objective of government

Government aims to allocate budgets to departments in a way that is aligned with its policy objectives and priorities, and provides certainty over budgeting in the short to medium term. Government also aims to provide clarity to citizens over the actions taken to use the resources allocated.

How this will be achieved

Since 1998, HM Treasury has carried out spending reviews to set firm expenditure limits and define the key priorities. Spending reviews are the government's key tool in medium-term expenditure planning. Spending reviews are also used as an opportunity to drive reform in how services are delivered, and to set the tone for engagement between HM Treasury and departments.

Our study

The study examined whether the spending review is effective as a medium-term spending and planning tool. It analysed the spending review process in the wider context of financial management in government, and against principles for robust decision-making.

Our evaluative criteria

The importance of spending reviews.

The Spending Review 2015 process.

Spending reviews as part of broader financial management.

The extent to which the Spending Review 2015 compared to principles for well-informed decision-making:

- Strong evidence on the cost and value of public services.
- A fully integrated view of public spending across organisational boundaries.
- A fully integrated view of public spending in the long term.
- A strong understanding of the capability to deliver change.
- 'Live' performance information to review success and hold to account.
- Transformation: a fundamental review of how to achieve outcomes.

Our evidence

(see Appendix Two for details)

The study team used different methods to examine aspects of the Spending Review, they:

- interviewed officials from HM Treasury, and other parts of the centre of government;
- undertook four case studies, and interviewed officials at the Department for Education, the Department for Transport, the Ministry of Justice, and the Department for Work & Pensions;
- met with key sector stakeholders;
- examined internal departmental documents;
- conducted an online survey of finance directors;
- reviewed existing literature and past NAO reports; and
- analysed quantitative spending data.

Our conclusions

The spending review process sets clear limits on departmental spending. This allows departments to plan for the medium term and align policy priorities with their budgets. HM Treasury has made some positive changes to the spending review process, including improvements in how it works with departments and other parts of the centre of government, such as the Cabinet Office. However, the process and supporting financial management system still do not make full use of the expertise within the centre of government, or incentivise collaboration across departments.

The way the spending review process works does not sufficiently address some fundamental issues with the way government functions. It also does not fully address previous concerns that we and the Committee of Public Accounts have raised. HM Treasury's approach remains rooted in bilateral negotiation. This allows it to function well as a control on departmental spending. However, it prevents the spending review from maximising the value for money of spending by tackling difficult and entrenched issues. These include both policy issues such as obesity and structural issues such as interdependencies between departments and the services they provide. Focusing on spending allocations and their consequences within just the spending review period reduces the attention paid to the longer term.

HM Treasury has made some progress in improving the spending review process, however it does not yet provide the best environment for achieving value for money. The spending review is undoubtedly a complex and difficult exercise. Improving the process and the wider engagement with departments would help HM Treasury to create a more mature planning and budgeting environment.

Appendix Two

Our evidence base

1 We reached our independent conclusion on whether the spending review is an effective mechanism for planning and allocating public money in the medium term by analysing evidence collected between February and April 2016.

2 We applied an analytical framework partly based on principles for well-informed decision-making. Our audit approach is outlined in Appendix One.

3 **We assessed the importance of spending reviews.**

- We conducted a **web survey** of finance directors in government departments to understand how they dealt with the Spending Review, and how it fitted into their wider financial management. The survey achieved an 82% response rate. It covered interactions with HM Treasury, questions on the long-term and cross-departmental dimensions of the Spending Review, and financial management.
- We **analysed spending data** to examine how financial plans made during spending reviews compare with actual outturns. We also analysed HM Treasury's data on capital spend and on its own workforce.

4 We **reviewed the extent to which the Spending Review 2015 looked at key issues**, based on our set of principles.

- We conducted **semi-structured interviews** with HM Treasury officials both in the General Expenditure Policy team and in the departmental spending teams for our case study departments. The interviews focused on the processes for reviewing submissions, relationships with departments, and the extent to which the Spending Review took a long-term and cross-departmental perspective.
- The study team selected **four case study departments**: the Department for Education, the Department for Transport, the Ministry of Justice, and the Department for Work & Pensions. Interviews with officials who worked on the spending team (mainly from the finance and strategy teams) focused on departments' preparations for the Spending Review 2015, any joint working between departments, and interactions with HM Treasury. This helped shed light on how the Spending Review aligned with our principles in practice.

5 We considered the **Spending Review 2015 process**.

- We conducted a **review of internal HM Treasury and departmental documents**. Documents reviewed included Spending Review submissions, internal timelines and project tracking documents, guidance to departments on preparing their Spending Review submissions, internal data, and communications between HM Treasury and departments.

6 We examined how spending reviews operate within **broader financial management in government**.

- We **interviewed different parts of the centre of government**, ranging from the Infrastructure and Projects Authority and the Crown Commercial Service to the Government Property Unit. This was to understand their role in providing expert support during the Spending Review. We met with key sector stakeholders to gather insights on the Spending Review and its strategic role. These stakeholders included the Institute for Fiscal Studies and the Institute for Government.
- We also **reviewed published material** on spending reviews and on financial management more broadly. This included a number of Organisation for Economic Cooperation and Development reports on budgetary processes globally. We drew on our past value-for-money reports, including *Managing budgeting in government*,[28] *Accountability to Parliament for taxpayers' money*,[29] and *A Short Guide to HM Treasury*.[30]

28 Comptroller and Auditor General, *Managing budgeting in government*, Session 2012-13, HC 597, National Audit Office, October 2012.

29 Comptroller and Auditor General, *Accountability to Parliament for taxpayers' money*, Session 2015-16, HC 849, National Audit Office, February 2016.

30 National Audit Office, *A Short Guide to HM Treasury*, July 2015.

Appendix Three

Evaluation of progress against the Committee of Public Accounts' recommendations

Figure 20

By April 2016, the government had made some progress on five of the Committee's seven recommendations from its 2013 report

Summary recommendation and government response	National Audit Office findings
1 HM Treasury and departments should identify, before each spending review, existing commitments and future funding pressures to make sure overall expenditure plans are realistic and sustainable in the longer term. The government agreed to implement the Committee's recommendation in time for a likely 2015-16 spending round. The response set out the high-level budgets which were protected, and that all commitments to significant expenditure in future spending review periods are subject to HM Treasury approval.	As set out in the government's response, high-level commitments to education, health, and overseas development aid (among others) were made before the Spending Review 2015, as well as to overall spending limits, which limited options for making changes during the Spending Review itself. At a lower level, in their initial submissions to HM Treasury, the four case study departments referred to existing manifesto commitments and the related funding requirements. Capital projects funded in the 2013 Spending Round were required to go through the same scrutiny as new ideas in Spending Review 2015.
2 Departments should model the financial and operational implications of different spending options to support their bids for funding in the next spending review. The government agreed to implement the Committee's recommendation in time for a likely 2015-16 spending round. This included departments being asked to model resource expenditure planning assumptions.	We saw evidence of departments and HM Treasury working together to understand the models and assumptions which underpinned bids before the Spending Review formally started. HM Treasury's guidance to departments for the Spending Review 2015 required them to provide two scenarios for spending reductions (25% and 40%). The majority of our case study departments did not do so, although in some cases this was agreed with HM Treasury before submission.
3 HM Treasury needs to enforce requirements for departments to assess the cost-effectiveness of their spending; analyse in aggregate how well departmental proposals address key government objectives such as growth and fairness; and work with Cabinet Office to make sure current information reforms reflect the need for informed budgeting. The government agreed with the Committee's recommendation and stated it had been implemented already, citing the business case process, the intended themes of the next spending review, and distributional impact analysis.	HM Treasury is working in this area, particularly through the Financial Management Review, although there is scope for additional efforts in this area. HM Treasury's Spending Review 2015 guidance and template asked departments to provide information on the relative value of their programmes: only one of the four formal submissions we reviewed did so. Some 10 of the 14 finance directors who responded to our survey said they completed the value-for-money assessment for only some or none of their programmes. Departments pointed out that HM Treasury's review of departmental bids for capital spending was opaque, and our review suggests that value-for-money considerations were sometimes left aside (for instance to fund a project with a negative net present value). HM Treasury attempted to benchmark costs in the area of operational expenditure, but there were significant gaps in the data departments provided.

Figure 20 *continued*

By April 2016, the government had made some progress on five of the Committee's seven recommendations from its 2013 report

Summary recommendation and government response	National Audit Office findings
4 HM Treasury, together with permanent secretaries, needs to address the technical and cultural barriers to joint working. This will include making sure that the budgetary system does not penalise departments bidding to increase budgets in order to lower overall government costs; and creating incentives for departments to pursue novel proposals which cross departmental boundaries. The government agreed with the idea of encouraging joint working across departments, with a target date of the 2013-14 financial year, but disagreed with the Committee's recommendation on departments bidding to increase budgets. HM Treasury sets out its work on Whole-Place Community Budgets and the Conflict Pool, and said it would assess how it can encourage and facilitate novel proposals on joint-budgeting within the existing framework.	HM Treasury recognises the importance of collaboration and acknowledged this recommendation. However, the spending review process does not enable cross-departmental issues to be dealt with in a unified manner. While the guidance provided by HM Treasury encouraged departments to consider joint bids, there were no explicit requirements for departments to set out their joint working. Only two formal joint bids were made in the Spending Review 2015, and although we know there were more examples of informal joint working this may not be sufficient for accountability. The government has created 11 implementation taskforces to take a cross-departmental view of major challenges and policy issues but not all of these issues were examined specifically at a cross-departmental level in the Spending Review.
5 HM Treasury should be clear about the skills it needs to be effective in challenging departments on their spending plans and subsequent performance, and put in a place a strategy to secure and retain staff with the appropriate skills and experience. The government agreed to implement the Committee's recommendation by April 2013, and points to work to restructure the department and monitor retention.	Some progress was made in terms of staff turnover in the spending teams since 2010. The Treasury made efforts to upskill its staff ahead of the Spending Review 2015. It also engaged internally, and with departments, early on to develop a robust understanding of departments' business and models. However, just over half of finance directors who responded to our survey felt that HM Treasury had sufficient capability to challenge their complete submissions robustly and in detail. All the other respondents felt that HM Treasury could challenge at least some of their submissions robustly.
6 HM Treasury should consider how it will establish effective mechanisms to enable departments to use previous experience across government in framing current and future programmes. The government agreed with the Committee's recommendation and stated it had been implemented already, citing specific examples of developing Private Finance 2 and the Commissioning Academy.	HM Treasury improved various aspects of budgeting, including planning and performance processes and reporting. We have not seen evidence to suggest that it has made other progress in making changes to the process based on any lessons learned from previous programmes to plan future spending.
7 HM Treasury should identify what information it could provide to select committees to enable them to scrutinise departmental spending plans and discuss with the Liaison Committee what might be done to encourage select committees to undertake this work. The government disagreed with the Committee's recommendation, stating that it already provides substantial opportunities for Parliament to scrutinise spending.	The government disagreed with this recommendation. The government has publicly stated its intention to make information linking spending and outcomes publicly available. The companion report to this publication focuses on single departmental plans, and found that the published plans do not make clear the link between funding and outcomes, and therefore fail to provide the public accountability we believe they should.

Source: National Audit Office

Appendix Four

Glossary

Figure 21
Glossary

Term	Meaning
Accountability	Accountability means being responsible for some action. For government this usually covers how resources, particularly taxpayers' money, are used, as well as whether the actions taken have the expected impact. Accountability usually requires giving an account – providing information on what has happened – as well as being held to account – having to answer for what has been done.
AME	Annually Managed Expenditure. Reflects volatile spending such as benefits payments, and can be subdivided into Resource AME and Capital AME along the same lines as DEL.
Business planning	Business planning refers to the more detailed process of setting out the resources an organisation has, how it works (its processes), how it will use its resources and processes to achieve the aims it set out, and how it will know if it is achieving those aims. It is likely to be carried out at all levels through an organisation, and to involve more short-term actions.
DEL	Departmental Expenditure Limit. For general running costs – split into the following (often referred to as 'control totals'):
Resource DEL (RDEL)	Pay or procurement or other expenditure often subdivided into administrative budget (support functions) and programme budget (frontline activities).
Capital DEL (CDEL)	Investment in assets such as buildings, equipment and land.
Strategic planning	Strategic planning refers to the organised process of defining an organisation's mission and aims, assessing its current state and the landscape in which it operates, and setting out at a high level how it intends to achieve its aims. It is likely to be carried by senior management, and to focus on a longer-term future and direction of travel.

Source: National Audit Office

Made in the USA
Monee, IL
08 May 2026

49761874R00033